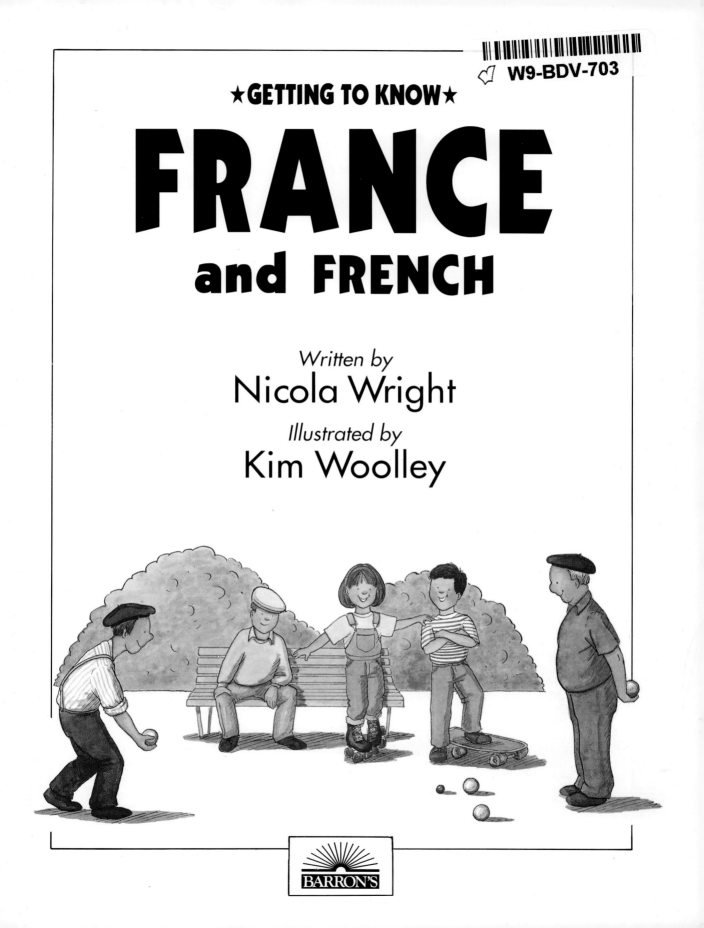

★GETTING TO KNOW★

FRANCE
and FRENCH

Written by
Nicola Wright

Illustrated by
Kim Woolley

W9-BDV-703

BARRON'S

Contents

First edition for the United States
published 1993 by Barron's Educational Series, Inc.

© copyright 1992 Times Four Publishing Ltd

First published in Great Britain in 1992 by
The Watts Group

All rights reserved.
No part of this book may be reproduced in any
form, by photostat, microfilm, xerography, or
any other means, or incorporated into any
information retrieval system, electronic or
mechanical, without the written permission of
the copyright owner.

All inquiries should be addressed to:
Barron's Educational Series, Inc.
250 Wireless Boulevard
Hauppauge, New York 11788

Library of Congress Catalog Card No.
92-38648

International Standard Book No.
0-8120-6336-8 (hardcover)
0-8120-1532-0 (paperback)

PRINTED IN HONG KONG

6   9907   987654

About this book

In this book you can find out about France — its people, landscapes, and language. For example, you will discover what the French like to eat and drink, what they do for a living, and what famous French places look like.

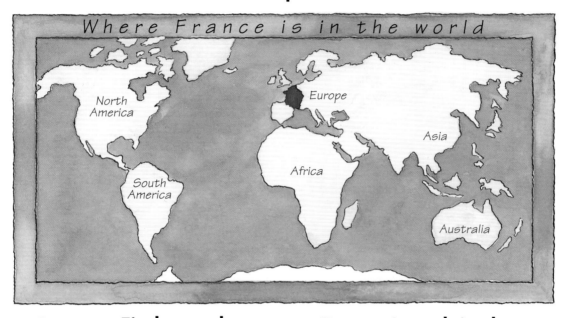

Where France is in the world

North America

Europe

Asia

Africa

South America

Australia

Find out, also, what school days are like for French children, and about their vacations and festivals. On page 26, there is a special section to introduce you to speaking French.

Hello!

Bonjour!

It explains how to use and pronounce everyday words and phrases, so you can make friends and ask for things in cafés and shops. Also, some French words and their meanings are given throughout the book to help you increase your vocabulary.

Map of France

France is one of the largest countries in Europe. It is bordered by seven other countries: Belgium, Luxembourg, Germany, Switzerland, Italy, Andorra, and Spain. Even so, almost half of France's border is coastline.

la carte
map

English Channel

Longest river:
The Loire, 634 miles (1,020 km). Many beautiful **châteaux** line its banks.

le fleuve
river

Corsica

The island of Corsica is part of France. It lies in the Mediterranean Sea, 100 miles (170 km) south of Nice.

The French landscape varies greatly. In some places there are high mountains and thick forests. In others, there are rolling fields and sandy beaches.

Diepp

Cherbourg

Le Havre

Roue

Caen

Normandy

St-Malo

Brest

Brittany

Rennes

Le Mans

Loire Valley

Loire

Nantes

Centre

Poitou-Charente

Lim

Limousi

Bordeaux

Dordogne

Garonne

Aquitaine

Midi-Pyrénées

Pyrenees

Spain

4

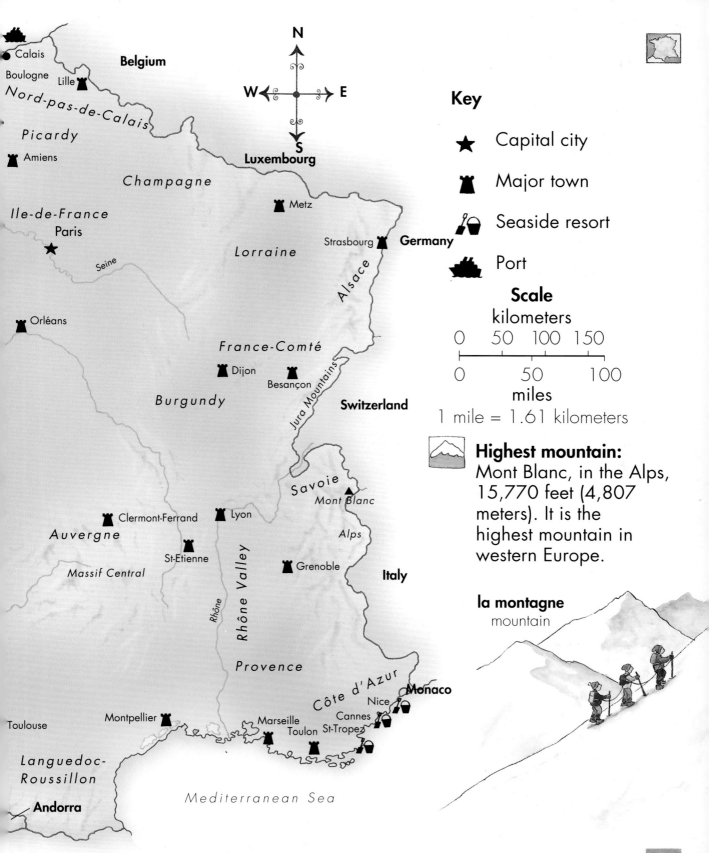

N
W E
S

Calais
Boulogne
Lille
Belgium
Nord-pas-de-Calais
Picardy
Amiens
Champagne
Ile-de-France
Paris
Metz
Luxembourg
Lorraine
Strasbourg
Germany
Alsace
Seine
Orléans
France-Comté
Dijon
Besançon
Jura Mountains
Switzerland
Burgundy
Savoie
Mont Blanc
Clermont-Ferrand
Lyon
Auvergne
Alps
St-Etienne
Grenoble
Italy
Massif Central
Rhône Valley
Rhône
Provence
Côte d'Azur
Monaco
Nice
Cannes
St-Tropez
Montpellier
Toulouse
Marseille
Toulon
Languedoc-Roussillon
Andorra
Mediterranean Sea

Key

★ Capital city

♟ Major town

⛱ Seaside resort

🚢 Port

Scale
kilometers
0   50   100   150

0   50   100
miles
1 mile = 1.61 kilometers

Highest mountain:
Mont Blanc, in the Alps, 15,770 feet (4,807 meters). It is the highest mountain in western Europe.

la montagne
mountain

Facts about France

Although France is about the size of Texas, almost three times as many people live there, so it is much more crowded.

Size: 220,668 sq miles (543,965 sq km)

Population: 56,555,700

This has been the French flag since the French Revolution in 1789. It is called the **tricolore** which means a flag with three stripes.

le drapeau
flag

The Head of State is the president, who is elected every seven years by the French people.

Language

Although the official language is French, there are other languages spoken in parts of the country:

la langue
language

Breton is spoken in the northwest. It is related to Cornish, Welsh, and Irish.

Basque is spoken in the region around the Spanish border. It is unlike any other European language.

German is spoken in Alsace and Lorraine, as these regions once belonged to Germany.

Money

French money is divided into **francs** (F) and **centimes** (ct). 100 centimes equals 1 franc.

l'argent
money

Bank notes are issued for the following amounts: 500, 200, 100, 50, and 20 francs. The heads of famous French people appear on the notes.

There are 10, 5, 2, 1, and ½ franc coins, and 20, 10, and 5 centime coins. The woman shown on the back of the coins is **Liberté**, representing freedom.

la pièce de monnaie
coin

le billet de banque
banknote

Capital city:
Paris

Official name:
La République Française
(French Republic)

Some things France is well known for

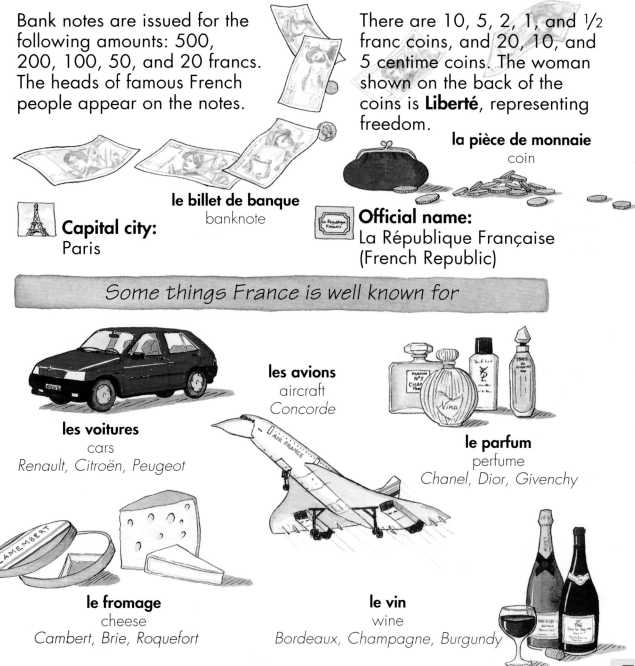

les voitures
cars
Renault, Citroën, Peugeot

les avions
aircraft
Concorde

le parfum
perfume
Chanel, Dior, Givenchy

le fromage
cheese
Cambert, Brie, Roquefort

le vin
wine
Bordeaux, Champagne, Burgundy

Regions of France

France is divided into many different regions, and includes the island of Corsica in the Mediterranean. The scenery, weather, and way of life vary greatly from region to region.

The north of France has cold winters, warm summers, and plenty of rainfall.

le temps
weather

le nord
north

le sud
south

In the south of France it is hot and dry in the summer and warm and sunny in the winter.

Many of the seaside resorts along the south coast, such as Cannes and Nice, were once small fishing ports. Now they are vacation places for people from all over Europe.

The French call the south coast the **Côte d'Azur**, which means "sky-blue coast," because of its good weather

le ski nautique
waterskiing

About one fifth of France is covered with forests. The Vosges and Jura mountains in the east are covered with pine and fir trees.

la forêt
forest

Wild animals, including boar, foxes, beavers, and chamois (a kind of antelope) can be found in these regions.

8

In the east, the high mountains of the Alps are covered with snow all year and the scenery is spectacular.

faire du ski
skiing

This region is very popular for skiing in the winter and hiking in summer.

la neige
snow

Normandy, in the north, has a flat coastline with long sandy beaches.

la côte
coast

la plage
beach

The coastline of Brittany in the northwest is rocky with many inlets.

Several large rivers run through the high, flat land of central France. Beautiful countryside and picturesque towns line their banks.

There are vineyards all over France. Most regions produce their own wine. Champagne and Burgundy are some of the best known.

le raisin
grape

le vignoble
vineyard

9

Paris

Paris is the largest and most important French city. It is the capital of the country and the center of industry, business, fashion, and entertainment.

The original city was built on an island in the middle of the River Seine. The island became known as the **Ile de la Cité** (City Island). During the twelfth century, the beautiful Notre-Dame cathedral was built on it.

Notre-Dame Cathedral

Paris is famous for its arts. There are many street painters in the district called Montmartre. Famous artists like Renoir and Picasso once lived there.

l'artiste
artist

The quickest and cheapest way to get around the city is on **le Métro** (the subway).

Over 10,200,000 people live in Paris and its suburbs, which is almost one fifth of the total French population.

les gens
people

RATP

10

Famous places

Palais du Louvre and the glass pyramids (art museum)

Sacré-Cœur
(church on top of the hill of Montmartre with splendid views of Paris)

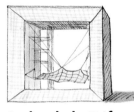

Arche de la Défense
(built to mark 200 years since the French Revolution)

Arc de Triomphe
(the Tomb of the Unknown Soldier is under it)

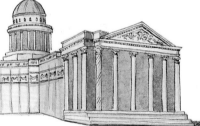

Panthéon
(church containing the tombs of some of those people who died during the Revolution)

Eiffel Tower
(built in 1889 for an exhibition)

Place de la Concorde
(many people were guillotined here during the Revolution)

Pompidou Center
(modern exhibition halls)

Moulin Rouge
(one of the most famous nightclubs in Paris)

In a typical French town

There is a square in the middle of most French towns and villages. All the main shops are grouped around it. Often there is a statue or water fountain in the center.

la boulangerie
bakery

le magasin
shop

People gather to talk in the main square under the shade of trees.

la charcuterie
delicatessen

le supermarché
supermarket

la poste
post office

Les agents de police patrol in the towns. **Les gendarmes** patrol the countryside. Both types of police wear a blue uniform.

l'épicerie
grocery store

la librairie-papeterie-maison de la presse
bookstore-stationers-newspaper shop

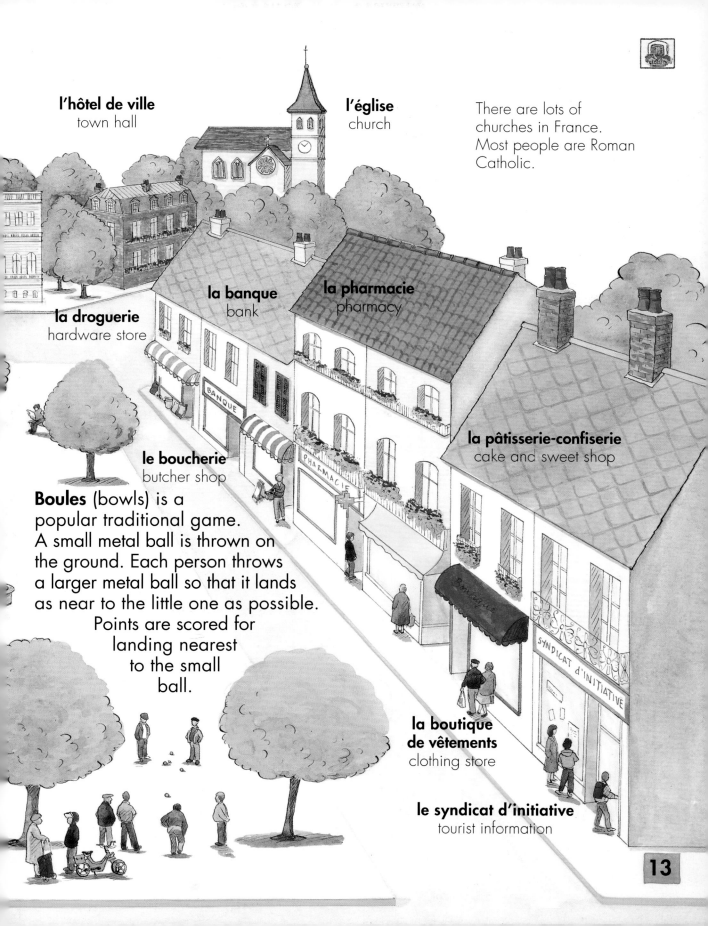

l'hôtel de ville
town hall

l'église
church

There are lots of churches in France. Most people are Roman Catholic.

la banque
bank

la pharmacie
pharmacy

la droguerie
hardware store

la pâtisserie-confiserie
cake and sweet shop

le boucherie
butcher shop

Boules (bowls) is a popular traditional game. A small metal ball is thrown on the ground. Each person throws a larger metal ball so that it lands as near to the little one as possible. Points are scored for landing nearest to the small ball.

la boutique de vêtements
clothing store

le syndicat d'initiative
tourist information

BANQUE

PHARMACIE

Boutique

SYNDICAT d'INITIATIVE

Eating in France

The French are famous for their love of food and cooking. Meals are never rushed and French restaurants are some of the best in the world.

Here is a typical French breakfast **(le petit déjeuner)** called a continental breakfast:

We drink our chocolate from bowls, and we like to dip bread into it.

la confiture
jam

le beurre
butter

la baguette
long French loaf

le café
coffee

le croissant
flaky, crescent-shaped roll

le chocalat chaud
hot chocolate

Here are some typical French dishes:

le bœuf bourguignon
a beef stew cooked in red wine

la quiche lorraine
bacon and egg custard

la salade niçoise

olives, anchovies, tomatoes, onions, and tuna fish

les crêpes
pancakes

les escargots
snails

la tarte Tatin
apple and custard pie

le pâté
pâté

les moules
mussels

Some well-known French drinks

l'apéritif
before-dinner drink
Pernod, Ricard

la bière
beer
usually made in Alsace

le cidre
cider

made in Normandy and Brittany

le vin
wine
Champagne, Burgundy, Muscadet

l'eau minérale
mineral water
Perrier (bubbly), Evian (still)

la liqueur
after-dinner drink
Kirsch, Chartreuse

A French meal

Lunch (**le déjeuner**) and dinner (**le dîner**) are usually large meals and can go on for hours.

le repas
meal

The meal starts with soup or **hors d'oeuvres** (appetizers). Next there is a meat or fish course. The salad is often eaten after this.

The meal ends with cheese, followed by a dessert or fruit.

15

What people do

France is a large country, and people live and work differently in the various regions. Some people work in busy industrial areas. Others live in the countryside and are farmers.

France is an important farming country, but today machines do much of the work. Fewer people now work on the land than in industry.

Farmers grow cereals (wheat, oats, and barley), grapes, fruit, and vegetables. Dairy farmers produce cheese, butter, milk, cream, and yogurt.

le fermier
farmer

French railways employ many people. France's **Train à Grande Vitesse** (TGV) runs between towns all over the country and holds the world rail speed record.

Sheep farming is common in the southeast and the central plateau. Roquefort cheese is made from sheep's milk.

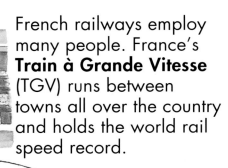

France is especially famous for its wine. The wine business employs many people, especially in the grape-picking season. The wines and brandies of France are sold all over the world.

le mouton
sheep

16

Steel, cars, shipbuilding, aircraft, textiles, perfume, and food products are some of France's main industries.

l'usine
factory

French farms and fisheries produce almost all the food the people need.

The people of Brittany (called Bretons) are mainly farmers and fishermen. Nearly half of the fish caught in the sea around France come from this region.

le pêcheur
fisherman

Figs, oranges, lemons, almonds, and olives are grown in the south, along the Mediterranean coast. Flowers are grown there, too, for making perfume. The perfume business is very important.

Many French people work in hotels and restaurants. There is an important tourist trade, especially in the Alps and along the Mediterranean coast.

Brasserie

Le Bistro

17

Children in France

Here you can find out something about school life in France, and about how French children spend their time.

l'école
school

The school day usually begins at 8:30 in the morning and lasts until 4:00 in the afternoon. There may be classes on Saturday mornings, but Wednesdays are normally free.

les vacances
vacations

School children have several long vacations. They get: one week at **Toussaint** (All Saints) which is the autumn mid-term; two weeks at Christmas; two weeks at the end of February (winter mid-term); two weeks at Easter, and two months in the summer.

les devoirs
homework

At most French schools, children do not wear a uniform. Many of them wear jeans, a sweatshirt, and sneakers.

les vêtements
clothes

Though French children have long vacations, many of them have to do **devoirs de vacances** (vacation homework), reviewing what they have learned at school during the year.

Many schools also offer what they call **classe de neige** (class in the snow) or **classe de mer** (class by the sea). The whole class spends a week in a ski resort or at the seaside. Lessons go on as usual, but the children also do outdoor activities.

All children take part in sports at school.

le sport
sport

> Athletics, gymnastics, and team sports such as football, volleyball, and basketball are played.

> One of the favorite pastimes of many French children is reading comics. Characters such as Asterix and Tintin are very popular.

le skateboard
skateboarding

As in many other countries, there are crazes. Over recent years these have included skateboarding and electronic games

la bande dessinée
comics

History of France

58 B.C.

The Romans, led by Julius Caesar, invaded France (or Gaul, as it was then called). It remained part of the huge Roman Empire for 400 years.

1066

le roi king

William the Conqueror (from Normandy, in northern France) invaded England, won the Battle of Hastings, and was crowned king of England.

1337–1453

During the Hundred Years War, England invaded France. The English won parts of France, but Joan of Arc inspired the French to rise up against them. She was captured by the English and burned to death in 1431. By 1453, the English had been defeated.

1789

In 1789, the French people decided to overthrow the king and nobles so the people themselves could rule the country. King Louis XVI, and many others, were beheaded. This was called the French Revolution.

le soldat
soldier

1804

Liberty leading the people
– a painting by Delacroix

1830–1848

Napoleon Bonaparte was a brilliant soldier, who became the people's hero during the French Revolution. He crowned himself Emperor in 1804. He was defeated by the English at the Battle of Waterloo in 1815.

After the Battle of Waterloo, the French royal family and nobles tried to return to power. However, they were defeated by the people in two more revolutions in 1830 and 1848.

1919

During World War II (1939–1945), Hitler's troops invaded France. General Charles de Gaulle led the French Resistance fighters who worked to defeat the Germans. France was eventually freed in 1944.

1944

France lost the regions of Alsace and Lorraine to Germany during the Franco-Prussian War in 1870. However, at the Treaty of Versailles at the end of World War I (1914–1918), Germany gave them back to France.

1958

In 1958, France joined with West Germany, Italy, Belgium, the Netherlands, and Luxembourg to form the European Economic Community.

21

Famous places

Thousands of tourists from all over the world visit France every year. There are many beautiful and interesting places to see. Here are some of them.

Near Paris is the enormous and magnificent royal palace called the Château de Versailles, built 300 years ago for King Louis XIV.

le pique-nique
picnic

Visitors picnic beside the many lakes, fountains, and statues on the grounds.

Mont-Saint Michel was built as a monastery on a tiny island off the coast of Normandy. When the tide is low, you can walk or drive to it across the sand.

l'ile
island

Annecy is a beautiful old lakeside town in the Savoie region. Visitors like to go boating on the lake.

le lac
lake

le pont
bridge

The Pont du Gard is a huge aqueduct in Provence, built over 2,000 years ago by the Romans. It carried spring water 21 miles (35 km) into the town of Nimes.

The old town of Rouen in Normandy has an important place in French history. It was here that Joan of Arc was burned to death by the English for leading the French against them. A monument marks where she was burned.

Jeanne d'Arc
Joan of Arc

The Château de Chambord, in the Loire Valley, is one of France's most extravagant châteaux. It has 440 rooms and a maze of staircases and turrets.

Corsica, a lovely island in the Mediterranean Sea, is a popular place for vacations. You can enjoy deep-sea diving in the clear, warm water.

la plage
beach

Festivals

The French love celebrations. Many festivals are held throughout the year. Some celebrate religious occasions and historical events, others the arts. Some regions have their own festivals.

On July 14, everyone in France celebrates the storming of the Bastille prison at the beginning of the French Revolution. There are torchlit processions, military parades, and firework displays. People decorate their houses with flags and dance in the streets all night.

la fête
festival

le festival du film
film festival

There are many festivals celebrating the arts, including theater, cinema, dance, and music. The International Film Festival, held in Cannes every year, attracts famous stars and filmmakers who come to see the year's new films.

In some parts of northern France, huge models of local historical heroes, called **Les Géants** (the giants), are paraded through the streets during special festivals.

At Christmas, people ski down the mountains at night carrying flaming torches.

le géant
giant

In the big wine-producing areas, local people celebrate the end of the grape harvest every autumn.

They hold dances and taste the new wine. Members of the wine societies dress up in traditional costume.

le cyclisme
cycling

The Tour de France is a cycle race that is held each summer. Cyclists from all over the world take part. Millions watch the race, either along the route or on television.

l'âne
donkey

On December 6, people in the north and east celebrate the Festival of St. Nicholas (Father Christmas), the patron saint of children. In many towns a man dressed as St. Nicholas walks through the streets with a donkey, handing out sweets to children.

On January 6, the French celebrate **la Fête des Rois** (festival of the three kings). People eat a special cake, and whoever finds the bean hidden in it is King of the Day.

Mardi Gras is an enormous carnival held in Nice. For 12 days people watch the processions of colorful floats and people in fancy dress.

You can join in a battle of flowers with the people on floats.

le char
float

le cortège
procession

25

Speaking French

You will find some useful, everyday French words on the following pages, plus some simple phrases that you can use to ask for things.

You will see that every word is written in three different ways:

une orange pressée —— these are the French words
(ewn or-AHN-zh preh-say) —— this gives you an idea of how to pronounce the French
orange juice

this is what it means in English

In each speech bubble you will find a French phrase, a guide to pronouncing it, and its English meaning. In the back of the book, you will find a Guide that will help you make the different French sounds. The best way to practice is by saying the words aloud—if possible, to someone who knows how to pronounce them correctly.

Je voudrais une glace —— the French words
(zhe voo-dreh ewn glas) —— how to pronounce the French words
I would like ice cream.

the English translation

Here are some easy French phrases to use when you want to make friends. Down the side of the page are other useful words and phrases that will be helpful in all kinds of situations.

Oui
(wee)
Yes

**Bonjour.
Comment t'appelles-tu?**
(bOHN-zh-oor. kum-AHN ta-pehl tew?)
Hello. What is your name?

**Je m'appelle
Mary. Et toi?**
(zhe ma-pehl ma-ree. ay twa?)
My name is Mary.
And yours?

Non
(nOHN)
No

S'il vous plaît
(seel voo pleh)
Please

Merci
(mehr-see)
Thank you

Bonjour
(bOHN-zh-oor)
Hello

**Où passes-tu
les vacances?**
(oo pahss-tew lay vak-AHN-ss?)
Where are you staying on
vacation?

J'habite là-bas.
(zh-abeet lah-bah)
I live over there.

Au revoir
(or-vwar)
Good-bye

Pardon
(par-dOHN)
Sorry

Excusez-moi
(ehks-kew-zay mwa)
Excuse me

Monsieur
(ms-yuh)
Mr.

Quel âge as-tu?
(kehl ah-zhe a-tew?)
How old are you?

J'ai douze ans.
(zh-ay dooz AHN)
I'm twelve.

Madame
(ma-dam)
Mrs.

Mademoiselle
(mad-mwa-zehl)
Miss

Parlez-vous anglais?
(parlay voo AHN-glay?)
Do you speak English?

27

At the café

un sandwich au fromage
(UHN SAHN-dweesh oh frum-a-zh)
cheese sandwich

le sel et le poivre
(le sehl ay le pwa-vre)
salt and pepper

une glace à la fraise
(ewn glas a la freh-z)
strawberry ice cream

Monsieur
(ms-yuh)
waiter

la carte
(la kart)
menu

un verre
(UHN vehr)
glass

Here you can see people ordering at a café using the phrase **Je voudrais,** which means **I would like.** Using this simple phrase you can order any of the items around the picture.

Qu'est-ce que je vous sers, Messieurs?
(kehs-ke zhe voo sehr, mays-yuh?)
What can I get you?

Je voudrais un sandwich au fromage et un Coca.
(zhe voo-dreh UHN SAHN-dweesh oh frum-a-zh ay UHN ko-ka)
I would like a cheese sandwich and a Coca-Cola.

un croque-monsieur
(UHN kruk ms-yuh)
toasted ham and cheese sandwich

une orange pressée
(ewn or-AHN-zh preh-say)
orange juice

des pommes frites
(day pum freet)
French fries

un sandwich au jambon
(UHN sAHN-dweesh oh zh-AHN-bOHN)
ham sandwich

une salade mixte
(ewn sa-lad meekst)
mixed salad

une glace au chocolat
(ewn glas oh shuk-u-la)
chocolate ice cream

Je voudrais une glace.
(zhe voo-dreh ewn glas)
I would like ice cream.

Madame
(ma-dam)
waitress

Quel parfum – fraise, chocolat ou vanille?
(kehl parf-UHN, freh-z, shuk-u-la oo va-nee-y?)
Which flavor — strawberry, chocolate, or vanilla?

l'addition
(la-dees-y-OHN)
bill

Monsieur! L'addition, s'il vous plaît.
(ms-yuh! la-dees-y-OHN, seel voo pleh)
Waiter! The bill please.

un Coca
(UHN ko-ka)
Coca-Cola

une glace à la vanille
(ewn glas a la va-nee-y)
vanilla ice cream

une carafe d'eau
(ewn ka-raf doh)
jug of water

un petit pain au chocolat
(UHN ptee pEHN oh shuk-u-la)
chocolate-filled pastry roll

les pommes de terre
(lay pum de tehr)
potatoes

les framboises
(lay frAHN-bwaz)
raspberries

les saucisses
(lay soh-seess)
sausages

le lait
(le leh)
milk

le pain
(le pEHN)
bread

les timbres
(lay tEHN-br)
stamps

la confiture
(la kOHN-fee-tewr)
jam

les bonbons
(lay bOHN-bOHN)
candy

les poissons
(lay pwa-ss-OHN)
fish

The children are shopping for fruit (les fruits) and vegetables (les légumes) in a grocery shop (épicerie-alimentation).

Puis-je vous aider?
(pew-ee-zh voo-zay-day?)
Can I help you?

Oui s'il vous plaît. Je voudrais un kilo de pommes.
(wee seel voo pleh. zhe voo-dreh UHN kee-lo de pum.)
Yes please. I would like one kilo (2 lbs) of apples.

le chou-fleur
(le shoo-flur)
cauliflower

le poulet
(le poo-leh)
chicken

la bande dessinée
(la bAHNd day-see-nay)
comics

Around the picture are some useful words for things you might want to buy in other shops using the same phrase **Je voudrais.**

les poires
(lay pwar)
pears

les œufs
(lay zuh)
eggs

le gâteau
(le gah-toh)
cake

le jouet
(le zh-oo-eh)
toy

les biscuits
(lay bee-skew-ee)
cookies

le journal
(le zh-oor-nal)
newspaper

Combien en voudriez-vous?
(kOHN-byEHN AHN voo-dree-ay voo?)
How many would you like?

Deux laitues, s'il vous plaît.
(duh leh-tew, seel voo pleh.)
Two heads of lettuce, please.

Index

un *(UHN)* 1   **deux** *(duh)* 2   **trois** *(trwah)* 3   **quatre** *(katr)* 4   **cinq** *(sEHNk)* 5   **six** *(seess)* 6   **sept** *(seht)* 7   **huit** *(ew-eet)* 8   **neuf** *(nuf)* 9   **dix** *(deess)* 10

janvier *(zh-AHN-vee-ay)* January

noir *(nwar)* black

blanc *(bl-AHN)* white

rouge *(roo-zh)* red

jaune *(zh-oh-n)* yellow

vert *(vehr)* green

bleu *(bluh)* blue

lundi *(lUHN-dee)* Monday

mardi *(mar-dee)* Tuesday

février *(fay-vree-ay)* February

mars *(marss)* March

avril *(avreel)* April

mai *(meh)* May

juin *(zh-ew-EHN)* June

juillet *(zh-ew-ee-ay)* July

août *(oot)* August

septembre *(sehpt-AHN-bre)* September

mercredi *(mehr-kre-dee)* Wednesday   **jeudi** *(zh-uh-dee)* Thursday   **vendredi** *(vAHN-dre-dee)* Friday   **samedi** *(sam-dee)* Saturday   **dimanche** *(deem-AHN-sh)* Sunday   **décembre** *(day-SAHN-bre)* December   **novembre** *(nuv-AHN-bre)* November   **octobre** *(uk-tub-re)* October